THE MAKING OF A BEAUTIFUL WEIRDO

NUGGETS TO PUSH THRU LIFE AND MAKE
THE AWKWARD BEAUTIFUL

T.C Mason, LICSW, LCSW-C

Edited by Iris Saunders of Iris Lenora Editing Services

For more information about special discounts for bulk purchases, bringing the author to your live event/book club meetings, professional workshops, therapy, and speaking engagements, please e-mail tcmason@imabeautifulweirdo.com

Instagram: imabeautifulweirdo
Twitter: @authortcmason
Website: www.imabeautifulweirdo.com

Cover and Interior design by Vanessa Mendozzi
www.vanessamendozzidesign.com

Printed in the United States of America

First Edition: June 2016
10 9 8 7 6 5 4 3 2 1

ISBN 978-0-9976572-0-3
ISBN 978-0-9976572-1-0 (e-book)

To my husband. I love you forever and a day. I am a fire and my flames are hotter and brighter because of you.
Thank-you for not smothering my fire.

To my children, you changed the game. What I thought I could become, became even greater because of you.
I love you.

To all that have felt out of place and or have been rejected for being themselves.
This is for you.

CONTENTS

"Day after day
after day
Night after night
after night
Tear after tear
after tear
I tried
I
I always tried
to put my best foot forward
But no matter what
it came off so awkward
But I ask myself
over and over again
why… "

"Beautiful Weirdo"
Beautiful Weirdo Mix-tape

INTRODUCTION

Who Am I? There are so many ways to answer that question. I could say I am a wife, mother, sister, daughter, friend, philanthropist, social worker, crafter, singer/song-writer, group exercise instructor, etc. The list could go on and on. But really, who am I after every action, accolade, and title has been stripped? I am a person who did not fit into a neat box. My peculiarities somehow always oozed out of the sides of the box. Sometimes that ooze was appreciated and other times it was the marker that separated me from others. Whether it was appreciated or not, they are some colorful experiences.

In fact, I find myself laughing randomly throughout the day when I remember various unsuspecting moments that have left indelible imprints on my life. These moments, filled with significant people, shaped and molded me for this present time. I am a mere representation of their crafty work and the vibrant personification of an old proverb; it takes a village to raise a child. Thus, I dare not say that I was self-made. Instead, I am a collection of experiences: a collection of lessons failed and learned, a collection of love, and a collection of sacrifices made, so I could learn and accept who I am. I am a *Beautiful Weirdo* – a person who accepts and enjoys the beauty and uniqueness of his or her own peculiarities.

This book is my "thank you" to those who knowingly and unknowingly curated pivotal moments of change. I am, because you are. So here's to the making of this *Beautiful Weirdo.*

"If I could hold on to time
like a mother
with her newborn child
never wantin
to miss one moment

If I could hold on to time
like a mother
with her newborn child
never wantin
to miss one moment…
Not even a litte bit"

"Hold on to Time"
Greenteasoul

BIG BEAR

One of my fondest memories is when my mother and I used to go to the movies together right after I had spent all day with her at her job. My mom was a medical transcriptionist and at that time I had no clue as to what that meant. All I knew was that my mommy listened to headphones and typed very fast. Whatever she was typing lasted for hours. I can still hear the clickety-clack of those old IBM keyboards and the voice in those headphones. After two hours of being at my mother's job, I was bored and eager to leave. By noon, I had already exhausted my imagination of every cartoon character that I could draw.

Bored out of my mind, and yet I was still charged with maintaining good behavior if I wanted the after work special. The after work special was the weekend treat of racing to the movie theater with my mother to catch a movie. We normally would get to the movie theater just in the nick of time. I think I enjoyed the rush and excitement of it all. Once settled, my mother would unload her big purse that held all of our snacks and treats. You see, my mother didn't believe in wasting money at the concession stand, so we would go to the store beforehand and load up her purse with treats. It was the most exhilarating feeling. Just thinking about it causes my lips to curl into a smile.

It's amazing how something so little brought the biggest joy. The reward of spending time with my mother at the movies motivated me to keep my behavior under control. I cherished that moment back then because it was pure fun, and now because I realize my mom's great sacrifice. I didn't know it then, but in hindsight, it must have been exhausting to work over eight hours and then take your child to the movies. My mother didn't complain or ever make our time together seem cumbersome. She did it with a smile, and for that I am grateful. She taught me to work hard and make sacrifices so I could play later.

***Beautiful Weirdo Nugget: *Hustle hard, sacrifice, and make time to play.*

*"I went to school
because I was smart
Graduated
Two degrees
and a lover of art"*

"Here I Am"
Beautiful Weirdo Mixtape

SMILING MEDICINE

It was my first job out of graduate school, and I must admit, I was extremely nervous. I had been away from my hometown of Washington, DC for six years pursuing my undergraduate and master's degree in social work. Now it was time to apply what I had learned in school to the real world. So, there I was, my first day as a treatment coordinator (i.e. new term for social worker) and I could hear my heart racing and feel panic overtaking me. I remember thinking, why is this happening to me?

I had taken a break to use the restroom, a single restroom in the center corner of our office floor. What I thought would be a quick restroom break, had turned into a nightmare threatening to smear my quest for the record as "model social worker." So I peeked out of the bathroom and tried inconspicuously to seek the attention of my female colleague who was sitting in the office across from the restroom. I gritted my teeth and whispered, "Hey, I used the toilet and it's coming back up. What do I do?" At that moment, I saw the whitest smile that I had ever seen in my life. The very sight of it made me feel better, however, the words that went along with that smile did not. My colleague with the grand smile said, "I don't know," and she continued typing on her computer. I went back to the restroom, grabbed the plunger and prayed,

"God, please don't let it go down like this!" The combination of the plunger and the prayer saved the day.

The funny thing is what I remember most about that situation is not the embarrassment or my heart feeling as though it was going to jump out of my chest. What I remember most is the grand smile on my colleague's face. Seeing that smile gave me a silent reassurance that everything was going to be okay. For that instant, it provided a quick calm, a reassurance that I could deal with the turds that were trying to overtake my mission to have a great first day and to be the best social worker that organization had ever seen.

That day I learned how smiling can be a healing medicine to people when given at the right time. Therefore, I adapted the habit of smiling more often. I started smiling at people when I would walk down the street, when I was taking public transportation, or wherever I would go. My thought was that my smile could be that one glimmer of sunshine that could let someone know that everything was going to be okay. I know what my colleague's smile meant to me when I felt like my world was overflowing (literally), and so I choose to pay it forward by demonstrating that same act every chance I get.

***Beautiful Weirdo Nugget:** *Smile, because my smile is healing medicine to this world.*

"See where I come from
it ain't all gravy
Walkin past people
hearin in their spirits
Lord save me
On every corner
of every block
I either know of someone
who's been shot
or been locked up
for pushin rocks
Dilapidated houses
So many mothers
but none with no spouses
And when I say
I come from Southeast
people start feeling
sorry for me"

"Who Would've Thought"
Dosage 2: Choices

CORNERSTONES

Not all of the lessons I've learned have come from my family and friends. Some of the lessons I've learned came from my encounters with three people who were passionate about their job of teaching. Their passion for teaching created the cornerstones of which would be the building blocks for my future decisions.

Cornerstone 1: Mrs. Wright

I met her in the third grade as a student

attending Benjamin Orr Elementary School in Southeast Washington, DC. Her name was Mrs. Wright. I can remember her face and how she was dressed, as everything about her resonated sophistication and class. She was an older African American woman with skin the color of Hershey's chocolate and a head full of short loose curls. Mrs. Wright was always neatly groomed. She wore blouses and skirts with stockings and sling back heels. She was the classiest woman I knew at that time.

Most of all, I remember that Mrs. Wright was a woman who demanded our respect and expected us to know our times tables. I remember how she would randomly call on us and we had to be ready to say our times tables, and if we weren't prepared, a hit with the ruler was the consequence. That was an awful lot of pressure for a third grader, but it was a surefire way to motivate us to learn and be ready to share what we learned. Preparation is a good lesson to learn early on, however that was not the only lesson Mrs. Wright ingrained in me. She ignited the fire in me to be great so that I could inspire others. The following incident is an example of how she did just that.

During class, we were challenged to do a certain activity. I don't recall the exact activity, but the reward was that you would get to go to Mrs. Wright's house. Motivated by this incentive, which was the biggest deal in the whole world, four or five girls (me included), rose to the challenge and won the special visit to Mrs. Wright's house. After school, we all saddled into Mrs. Wright's car, and I took in every detail along the drive. Then, just as we were pulling up to Mrs. Wright's house, the life changing moment happened. She clicked a button from inside of her car and her garage door lifted. I thought to myself, this is definitely the flyest woman that I had ever met; she has automatic doors in her house. It was then when I decided that I had to have a house fully equipped with an automatic door. I just had to be a fly lady like Mrs. Wright who dressed classy, demanded respect, and could make things move at the touch of a button.

Now that I'm older, it seems funny as I reflect upon my thoughts as a third grader. Needless to say those moments shaped me. They showed me that there were African American women who were professional and owned nice things. These moments were a stark contrast to what I saw in my Southeast, DC neighborhood, where a lot of the African American women were unfortunately known as drug addicts. I decided then, in the third grade, that I would be like Mrs. Wright and not like some of the women in my neighborhood.

Just as Mrs. Wright exposed me to a world outside of my poverty-stricken neighborhood, I have made it a point to do the same with others. On one of my past jobs, I took a young girl to my house and she was amazed that I had my own house. I saw a light spark in her eye, when she asked, "This entire house is yours?" It was the same light I had as a third grader when Mrs. Wright had pulled up to her house and pressed her garage door opener. It was the moment when you understood that if this is possible for her, than this is also possible for me.

***Beautiful Weirdo Nugget:** *We are all lights and torches. Therefore, it's important to share our light with others, as we never know what that spark may become.*

Cornerstone 2: Mrs. Lee

I have always loved school and learning, and because of that, I did well academically. However, my smart mouth and or poor attitude tended to minimize my academic achievements at times. I took pride in my work and having good behavior, but I also had to have the last word in all situations.

My desire to have the last word didn't go over well with my teacher, Mrs. Phyllis Lee. As you can imagine, having the last word got me into trouble. And in Mrs. Lee's class, getting into trouble resulted in your name being written in the Bad Behavior Book. The Bad Behavior Book was the big bad book of doom. In my opinion it was the worst thing that could happen to any student. I hate to say it, but it happened. Mrs. Lee instructed me to do something and I did the opposite of what she had told me to do. As a result, I was told to leave the class and stand outside of the classroom.

There I was, peering in from outside the window of the classroom door. That was the ultimate torture for a nerd. When I could no longer stand it, I had the bright idea to tap on the door's glass window to get Mrs. Lee's attention. Surely, she would let me in. Mrs. Lee came to the door and slightly pulled it ajar. I don't remember what she said, but she didn't let me back into the classroom. I did what I thought I had to do. I tried to push my way in thru the little door opening. Mrs. Lee stood her ground, and I could, in no way, get past her and her healthy and majestic stature. Consequently, I was entered into the dreaded Bad Behavior Book.

Adding more pain to the torture, I had to write my own name in the Bad Behavior Book. I hated it and was so embarrassed.

Nonetheless, the bad deed had been done. I thought that was the end of my world and I was doomed to a life of bad behavior. It's amazing how out of proportion things seemed in that moment. I can laugh now, but I wasn't laughing then. I thought that cloud of doom would hover over my head forever.

Finally, the end of the day came. I remember Mrs. Lee would let some of the girls stay after school to help her clean up or do other things. I loved staying after school to help Mrs. Lee for anything, as I was a latchkey kid and those moments soaked up the time before my mother would come home from work. This was probably the only time I took joy in cleaning up (lol). It was interesting that, even after my behavior earlier that day, I stayed after school to help her erase the chalkboards and tidy up our classroom.

She took me home after we cleaned up

and I found myself still walking on eggshells because of the poor choice I made that day. She told me that she was disappointed because I had made a poor choice and that she knew I could do better. Her loving correction meant the world to me. It let me know that I was not "bad" but that I had simply made a poor choice and could do better. Mrs. Lee didn't hold my behavior over my head as to condemn me to damnation. Instead, she gently encouraged me to do and be better. I'll have you know that was the first and last time I ever wrote my name in that Bad Behavior Book.

Now that I am older, this experience is something I try to keep at the forefront of my memory as it concerns my relationships with others. People make poor choices, but that does not entitle them to be labeled "bad people." Thank you, Mrs. Lee, for giving me another chance.

***Beautiful Weirdo Nugget:** *Yes, you've made poor choices, but it doesn't mean you should label yourself, or allow anyone else to label you as "bad." You can always do and be better when you decide you want to do and be better.*

Cornerstone 3: Mrs. Lindsay

She personified everything it meant to be a sophisticated grown woman. Through my child eyes, I declared, a grown woman wears heels and her expensive perfume leaves an aroma as evidence of her presence. I can still hear the clicking of her heels against the tiled hallway as her sixth grade class walked to the restrooms. The sounds of her heels signaled "I am woman, hear me roar!" I practiced the same saunter over and over at home, though I didn't quite master it. I don't think anyone could get that clean, walking in heels sound. And, might I add the beautiful scent of her perfume lingered with every step she took. She, indeed, met all of the classifications of a "grown woman." I admired her dearly.

Mrs. Lindsay was an expert in my book. So when graduation came and we had to say goodbye to our friends and teachers, I had to have her sign my yearbook. She signed, "May you prosper in every endeavor you choose to undertake." My first thought was, "Mrs. Lindsay is so intelligent" and my second thought was, "I am so special because she used a big word (endeavor) in my yearbook." According to the Merriam-Webster dictionary, endeavor is an attempt to achieve. I don't know if this was a general departure greeting that Mrs. Lindsay wrote to all of her students, since I didn't check my classmates' yearbooks. What I do know is, I have never forgotten those words and often share them with others as birthday wishes and words of encouragement.

Mrs. Lindsay left me with words of encouragement to encourage myself and now I use those same words to encourage others. Oh how powerful words are, as they can be passed on to uplift others or passed on to destroy others.

***Beautiful Weirdo Nugget: *With my words I can pass on a blessing of encouragement that can travel from generation to generation and impact nations. With my words I can pass on a curse of discouragement that can travel from generation to generation and impact nations. Oh, our words have power.*

The sweetest woman I know
is a woman who'd give
her heart and soul
to people she
barely even know
She's so sweet…
sweeter than a honeycomb
The sweetest woman I know..."

"Honeycomb"
Greenteasoul

HONEY

Her name is Helen B. Scott, but they call her "Honey." I never really got the story behind her nickname, but if I had to guess, it's probably the obvious; she is so sweet. I'm not talking the kind of sweet that you find in lollipops, gummy bears, ice-cream cones, or fairies. No, she is not that kind of sweet at all. Considering, this is the same woman who knocked my teeth out for disrespecting her in church (now, don't get all riled up or call child protective services on her, my teeth were already loose). The same woman, who at the age of 70, helped my uncle lift my heavy 36-inch, CRT television onto my college storage unit.

My grandmother (whom I affectionately call Grahammy) and is affectionately known to others as, "Honey," is definitely a different kind of sweet. Her sweetness isn't in the words that she says, because I find that she is rather stern with her words. But her sweetness is in her actions and in how she shows her love for others.

Ever since I was child, I can remember countless acts of my Grahammy's kindness. We would be walking to the bus stop and my grandmother would pick up a toy on the ground, take it home, and clean it up to give to someone who needed toys. Often, I would come home from school and find a new person who had taken residence on my Grahammy's sofa. People always knew that if you went to Grahammy's house, she would not turn you away. Neighborhood drunks even came to my Grahammy's house. She saved the leftover food so that they could have something to eat. She is that kind of sweet, where she sacrifices her wants or needs to ensure that the needs of others are met. She believes in doing what is right, and her deposits of kindness and integrity found their way into my life.

I was eight or nine years old when my Grahammy and I went to People's Drug store; you all probably know this store by its new name, CVS Pharmacy. We went in to get a treat or something before we would ride the routine 32 bus, which would take us within walking distance of her house. Just as we saw the 32 bus inching to the bus stop, my Grahammy realized that she had carelessly walked out of the store without paying for a box of tissue that was still clenched in her hand. I saw the bus come to a stop, so I begin to head in its direction to board it, however, before I could get a good walking stride, my Grahammy ushered me back into the store. As my Grahammy stood in line to pay for the box of tissue, I saw the bus roll down the street, headed towards its destination…without us.

I couldn't believe it. We had missed our bus all because my Grahammy just had to go in and pay for the box of tissues. I was upset that we missed our bus for a box of tissue. I expressed my feelings to my Grahammy, "Geez grandma, it was only a dollar!" She replied, "I know. I forgot to pay for it." I thought my Grahammy was too old to get it, but really it was me who didn't get it.

There was another time when I thought my Grahammy was absolutely, positively freaking nuts for her suggestions. I was 13 years old, working my first summer job, (thanks to Former DC Mayor, Marion Barry) when I had found a person's purse that contained their check and their ID card for their summer job. Immediately I thought I was rich. I found their check and their ID card, which meant I could cash in on some extra money. In my excitement, I told my Grahammy about my great luck, but she didn't respond like I'd hoped. Grahammy instructed me to find the owner and return their belongings.

Surely I thought my Grahammy had lost her mind. Needless to say, I located the young lady, just like my Grahammy told me to do. I didn't want to do it but I did. I gave up the purse, the wallet, and the ID begrudgingly. My Grahammy didn't give me any huge accolades for following her instructions. To her, it was a fabric of life to be kind and a person of integrity. Those moments were impressionable for me. And though my Grahammy didn't say much, her actions spoke volumes.

As an adult, I have had many situations where I could see my Grahammy's honey oozing out of me. Just recently, a situation presented itself where I could have had an extra $210.00 in my pocket. I was picking up the mail from one of my jobs when I noticed an envelope that had a blank money order inside for $210.00. You may be wondering what I did. I thought about how I would feel if I had lost that amount of money. I would have been very upset! With all that in mind, I let my Grahammy's honey flow right through me and put on my detective hat to figure out how to find the person who lost the money order. I figured out that they probably used an envelope from their job, so I called the phone number on the heading of the envelope. Sure enough, the person I was looking for worked there. So I tracked her down and linked up with her to give her the money order. I found joy in that act, knowing that I had sown a seed of goodness and kindness. Honey flows through me now because I have learned so much from her acts of kindness.

***Beautiful Weirdo Nugget:** *I come from a lineage of sweetness and I learned from Queen Honey, my Grahammy, that my actions are my honey. I can make sweet the sourest situations. Use your honey wisely.*

"Inspire
me
to
be
the
higher me
Let
me
know
it's worth it
to
dream"

"Inspire"
Dosage 1: Shades of Green

GUMMYBEAR

I was at a singles seminar at church and we were learning auto mechanics, how to maintain your car, and how to change a tire. Me, being the woman I am, I thought it was essential that I knew how to change a tire and take care of my car. After all, what is sexier than a woman who's good looking and can change a tire on a car? The sight of that would surely capture a man's attention, right? So, I figured this was the seminar for me. And there she was, standing across from me, wearing a green military jacket, and gloating about how she already knew how to change a car tire. "Go figure! She already knows how to change a tire," I thought to myself. She nonchalantly explained that she was only there because it was the better of the seminars being offered at that time.

By now, I'm wondering who this chick is because I had never seen her at church. So I did what I thought was the right thing to do, I paid her a compliment to break the ice, introduced myself, and made an undercover attempt to confiscate her jacket. I said, "That's a nice jacket, is that mine?" She laughed and told me her name. I don't know what it was but I was naturally drawn to her. She seemed to be carefree and enjoying life as a Christian. At that time, I was not enjoying being a Christian at all. It sucked. I enjoyed singing in church, but other than that, I found it boring, lonely, and confining. But this chick, she seemed to be happy and having fun in her life as a Christian. On top of all that, I found out she could sing too. I silently thanked God for the answer to my prayers. That was the start of our friendship.

As we hung out together, the more I learned that I was not the only person who was drawn to her. She had a host of friends and they were all different. It seems that she had the "it" personality that attracted all different kinds of people. She was and is my friendly Gummybear. She is the treat very few people resist or dislike, the neighborhood comfort candy, the handy snack at the movies, my Gummybear.

Her personality is warm, and never condescending, no matter if one had done something displeasing. She understands connections and I believe she is gifted at

connectedness and maintaining her relationships. She knows how to honor individuals'
strengths instead of disconnecting from them
because of their weaknesses. This is the "it"
factor of my friendly Gummybear. People
flock to her because of her warmth, empathy,
and patience during challenging times. I have
met very few people like this; in fact, I only
know of one other person. When I look at
my friendly Gummybear and look at myself,
I am definitely a stark contrast.

I have always been the kind of person who
loves groups, but quickly disregards people
for one reason or another. I have very few
friends and even fewer close friends. However,
being a friend of the friendly gummy bear has
shifted my perspective. I have seen first hand
how she demonstrates and cultivates the love
in her relationships. It is through witnessing
her interactions and relationships with others

that I have learned how to love all different kinds of people. More importantly, she has showed me that I can love and respect differences, while still upholding my personal values. If someone has different values, that doesn't mean I have to separate myself or put them on the outskirts. I learned that from Gummybear. It is one thing to read the Bible that commands us to love others, but it is another thing to actually see it illustrated in a person's life.

***Beautiful Weirdo Nugget:** *Everyone doesn't have to be exactly like you to be your friend. Be warm and respect the Beautiful Weirdo inside of us all.*

"I'm sittin here
thinking bout life
what I've seen
what I've heard
And now more than ever
I must
protect
and guard
my heart

Sticks and stones
may break your bones
but those words
will never hurt you
That's the story that's told
but it ain't true…"
I guess that's why I got to
protect my heart"

"Protect my Heart"
Greenteasoul

WORLD OUTSIDE
MY WINDOW

Window I

I met her in church and we were both broken. My drug of choice to aid my pain was male companionship and hers was control. We were good at confiding in one another as we shared common interests in God, music, and pain. Our worlds were drastically different though. During that time, when I was stressed or depressed, I would disconnect from life.

I didn't want to talk to anyone, so I would shut myself off. When she was stressed or depressed, she wanted to connect and talk. I had been taking my self-preservation missions for so long, that I hadn't even thought about how it affected others. That soon changed.

As a first time homebuyer, I found myself at Lowes bombarded by a million choices for the color of orange. It was during my sensory overload when she called. I looked down at my phone and ignored her call. She called more than once and I ignored her call each time. I did not want to be bothered. I did not feel like talking to her. I wanted my space to be alone. I was overwhelmed. The last ignored phone call, was the straw that broke the camel's back. My friend expressed her anger with me, and boy did she let me have it. I can still hear the furious and matter of fact tone in her voice when she yelled, "You can't just check out like that....what if I really needed you? You're selfish and you only care about yourself!" Her words hit me like a ton of bricks. They were painful to hear and painful to digest. I had never had anyone to talk to me that way, nor to call me out on the carpet. I had to come to terms with how my behavior of protecting myself was harming others. This experience was the beginning of a long road of self-discovery and healing.

Although we were able to mend some of the expectations for our friendship, our relationship was never the same. I often wish I could have a do-over with her and try our friendship again. However, even if we had a do-over, the results would be much of the same because we were both responding from hurt places. She was responding from hurt because I represented the people in her life who were unreliable and selfish. I was responding from hurt because I went into self-preservation mode when things seemed overwhelming. That experience impacted my life and my relationships. I answer calls from my close friends to see if I'm needed or if they simply want to talk. If necessary, I share when I am feeling overwhelmed.

***Beautiful Weirdo Nugget:** *Do not be a thief. Do not rob people of their choice to be in your circle when things are overwhelming. It is their right to choose to bear your gripes and it is your choice to let them in.*

Window II

I was just about to perform at a gig when I received a phone call from one of my girl-friends telling me she did not want to be my friend anymore. It was a friendship breakup. I was in utter disbelief as she went on to explain that, in comparison to her works of love, she felt as though I didn't do enough for her during our friendship. She mentioned a time when I was in a car accident and she picked me up from the scene of the accident and took me home. She did not recall me being appreciative by telling her "thank you" for helping me. Then she mentioned another time when she made me a cup of tea and I expressed that I did not like the flavor of the tea. All of this was news to me, as she had not previously mentioned any of these things in our discussions.

I felt blind-sided and hurt that she viewed me as a taker and selfish. I was so shocked that I didn't respond to her accusations. At that time, I didn't believe in justifying friend-ships by keeping a record of everything that I did for my friends. A piece of me still doesn't believe in doing that. Instead, I held the belief that once I have let you in, you become my family. Family doesn't keep a record book of what they do for each other; they just do it because they're family.

However, those are my beliefs. My beliefs did not take up the slack that her needs weren't being met in our friendship. I learned many lessons about friendship from our breakup. I learned to always check in with your friends to ensure that you're on the same page. I randomly ask questions like, "How can I be a better friend to you?" I try to identify their love language so that I value them the way they like to be valued, not in the way I like to be valued. It makes a big difference.

I also learned to randomly share with my loved ones how much I appreciate their presence in my life. I don't ever want them to leave this earth without knowing how much their life has meant to me. So although the loss of her friendship was painful, the lessons I learned have added depth and appreciation to the relationships that I have in my life.

***Beautiful Weirdo Nugget: *Good friends are precious and priceless. They have the power to be life-long assets that can mature into timeless beauties when you nurture and appreciate them in the way that is meaningful to them.*

Picture Window

I am a child of a parent who has struggled with alcoholism for the bulk of my life. Witnessing their struggle with alcoholism, throughout my childhood, had an impact on my perception of the world. What I deemed as normal for my family wasn't normal in the world outside my window. It wasn't the gum-drops and lollipops *Candy Land* kind of world. It was a volatile world, with a sole focus of surviving from day to day. And when you're only focused on surviving, everything outside your window is a blur. Nothing stood out, so I created cautionary yellow tape and red stop signs as perimeters and barriers to protect me from getting hurt. To me, having barriers was so normal that I had become blind by the good actions and intentions of other people.

***Beautiful Weirdo Nugget:** *Don't live through the window of your past, it skews your view. Living in the past is like looking in the distorted mirror at the carnival's Funhouse. Things appear to be one way, but they really aren't. Take the risk and be vulnerable. Remove the yellow tape. Choose to trust again while relying on God to be your safety net.*

"I got you
You got me
We got us
So let's just be
like
Help out each other
Work with each other
Pray for each one another
We can do it if we try"

"Let's Just Be"
Dosage 3: Choices

HOLIDAY LOVE

Most of my memories regarding the holiday season are summed up in two words, holidays suck. I especially hated Thanksgiving and Christmas, the two biggest family oriented times of year. During those times, I felt like the biggest orphan in the world. My mother would work during the holidays, because she got double pay, and rarely was there a plan for where I would go to celebrate. It was left up to me to find somewhere to go.

Most of the times my Grahammy was

invited places and I would try to tag along with her. But having no place to go was never a good feeling. The older I got, the worse it was for me tagging along with my Grahammy. I discovered that people were more tolerant of a child tagging along than some random adult. It had gotten so bad that I would become depressed around the holidays, which made me more apt to making poor choices in the haze of that depressive funk.

All that changed in the fall of 2004. Somehow I got invited to my co-worker's parent's house on Thanksgiving. I remember arriving to the house and seeing a holy cross trimmed with white Christmas lights in their window. When I walked in the house, I could feel the warmth and positive energy flowing. It was matched with a glaring bright smile and a great big hug from LeJoi Montgomery. Her embrace was therapeutic. I felt like I was a long lost child who had just found her way home.

I really enjoyed myself that night. I had so much fun! I laughed, ate (LeJoi is a wonderful cook), and laughed some more. There was no tension in the air or awkwardness. I had never felt so comfortable on a first visit anywhere. Her husband, Wayne Montgomery, and the rest of the family were so welcoming. I was at home. I felt so at home that I spent the night. The next day, my co-worker called from our job to have a general conversation with her mom and discovered that I was still there (eating homemade sweet potato cake and drinking tea) with her parents. It was hilarious. It was the best Thanksgiving ever and the beginning of my love for the holidays!

As I reflect on when I first arrived at the Montgomery's house, I could not identify what it was that made their house such a home. Now I realize their home was anointed and I could sense the peace of God there. The peace of God permeated their home so much that I did not want to leave. To this day, if you enter feeling sad and broken, you will leave feeling happy and restored. That is literally what happened to me. I came in broken and depressed, and was transformed from a person who hated the holidays to a person who loves and looks forward to the holidays. I haven't missed one Thanksgiving since that first one at the Montgomery's. In fact, I try to get other people to join me, especially those who may feel alone on the holidays or struggle with depression.

The lessons I have learned from LeJoi and Wayne Montgomery (affectionately called Mom and Pop Pop Montgomery) are invaluable. It is because of them that the holidays are no longer gloom and doom, but they are beautiful moments to make memories with family.

***Beautiful Weirdo Nuggets:

1. As children, we are born in to families, but as adults, we have the power to choose our families; which is not relegated to biological bloodlines. Who you call your family is your choice, so choose wisely. 2. Darkness cannot stay where there is light. Run, create, and stay in the light, and eventually you will be a torch for others.

"I see you
left
and did your own thing
Had to see
if
what
you
had
was really what you wanted
Findin out that the world's
not
what its cracked up to be
They didn't even
see
your true value
like me"

"Come Back"
Dosage 1: Shades of Green

DEAR GOD

My Grahammy introduced me to God at an early age. As a part of her babysitting me, I had to go to church with her all the time. I hated it. There were no children there and because I had to attend church with my Grahammy, I missed out on playtime with my friends. I went to church with my Grahammy until I was capable of supervising myself. However, as soon as I got to the age where I felt free, I was forced to attend church again. This time, it was my mother who made me attend church. Though I initially had a sour attitude about going, I eventually warmed up to the idea.

I accepted Jesus Christ as my Lord and Savior when I was in the sixth grade. I remember the highs of being excited, hopeful and overzealous about trying to get everyone "saved." I can also remember the lows of being ostracized in high school, college, and adulthood for my peculiar behavior. I was young and did not understand the context of things, so I took everything literally and tried to do everything perfectly. I even stopped cursing and put forth the best effort not to kiss boys (that didn't work out so well for a middle school girl, but I tried). By the 10th grade, I had stopped dating boys, stopped going to parties, or doing anything I perceived was against my Christian beliefs. I spent my time in church and participating in the church's youth program and I had a good time, but things became more complex as I got older.

In the 12th grade, I decided that I wanted a boyfriend, but by that time I had already had a reputation for not "putting out" and for being a Christian, so that didn't quite work out. When I went away to college, the University of Pittsburgh, it was much of the same. I didn't go to parties (other than the two freshman mixers), didn't drink, was a virgin, and I was sad and lonely. I spent a lot of time in my room. I wrote poems and songs, and talked to God sporadically.

At some point I just stopped talking to Him because I was angry with Him. My relationship with God would continue like that for a while. I had periods of being a devout Christian, but it was during those periods where I felt ostracized the most. I remember being called names like "Mary Mother of God," or

"Grandma" in college. It was funny to those who called me those names, but it wasn't funny to me. I really wanted to belong, but I felt like I was caught between two worlds. I wasn't secular enough to fit in with "the world," yet I wasn't "super saved" enough to fit in with the Christian folks.

The Christian folks had too many rules and I wasn't good at keeping them. I constantly felt like a failure. I felt like after all God had done for me, I just kept letting Him down…so I'd just say forget it. Then I would try again. As I matured, I threw out a lot of the "if you're saved, you don't do this" kind of rules. Instead, I went on a quest to figure out how my relationship with God worked.

I had to learn for myself what God means to me. I learned that my relationship with God is more than adhering to rules. It is a relationship based on the foundation of unconditional love. God accepts me, flaws and all, and since God accepts me, I accept myself. Even when I don't make the best decisions (I know that's hard to believe), I continue to love me and press on through life. I continue to communicate with God. I know for myself, that God loves me. Therefore, I don't give up and I don't quit.

*****Beautiful Weirdo Nugget:** *Don't try to establish a relationship based upon other people's spirituality or relationship with God. Relationships are not cookie cutter. The guidelines that people have set for their lives doesn't necessarily make them adaptable to your life. Every individual is unique, fearfully and wonderfully made. God wants to know you. He will meet you where you are. He loves you unconditionally.*

"Have you ever
said a prayer
believed a prayer
forgot
all
about
it
'til it showed up there
Now you're in disbelief
'cause the words you speak
now you see"

"Touched a Prayer"
Beautiful Weirdo Mixtape

FATHER

I longed for my father. Always. I remember my mother would tell me stories about my biological father; she said he could cook, sing, and dance. She also mentioned that he was an exotic dancer too (note: some things you probably shouldn't share with your children at a young age). I internalized what my mother shared with me about my father. I thought, since he is a great singer, chef, and a dancer, then so am I. It's my destiny to become those things (stripper included)! I wanted to be like my father and carry a resemblance that I was his seed, his child. What I didn't know was that I wanted to be like a person who would be absent and not play an active role in their child's life. Unfortunately, I desired a relationship with him that went starved. My father's absence in my life deeply affected me in ways I could never imagine.

During my childhood, I prayed to God for a father over and over again. At the age of six years old, I had crying fits because I didn't have a father. My mother didn't understand it. She would say things like, but you have Uncle so and so, as her sincere attempt to console me. However, I was surrounded by people who had their father in their lives, including my cousins and friends. Observing the relationships they had with their fathers was a constant reminder that I didn't have mine.

I only have two memories of my father.

One memory, from when I was about seven years old, is of us walking back from Wah Sing restaurant. He declared he would be an active part in my life (lie #1). The other memory is from when I was in junior high school. He had promised to buy me the things I needed for a fashion show (lie #2). He never bought me those things and it angered me. So, I did what I knew to do; I unleashed the wrath of a fiery adolescent, and ended my rant with words like, "I want nothing to do with you" and "Never call me again!"

Though our last verbal encounter was one filled with anger, lashing out, reminding him of broken promises and giving him "a piece of my mind," my heart was broken. Contrary to the dismissive words spoken, I still wanted my father. I interpreted his lack of involvement as abandonment and that something had to have been wrong with me to make my father leave me. I began to believe the notion that people would always leave me.

Regardless of all those negative beliefs, I began searching for my father. Not actually searching for my biological father, but considering any male my mother dated to be my father. I remember my mother dating this guy for a while and when their relationship ended, I was crushed. I thought, thanks a lot, mom, for ruining my chances of having a father. Though my mother's relationship with her romantic partner didn't last, I still believed that God heard my prayer for a father and I still expected my "I need a father" prayer to be answered via my mother's relationship with a man. It was not.

Just when I thought God had forgotten about me, He answered my prayers. I was 13 when I met him or should I say them. They had just gotten married. I was in the crux of one of the most difficult developmental stages, adolescence, while also being forced to attend church. They were deeply involved in the music ministry of the church that my mother was forcing me to attend. Although I didn't want to attend the church and had vowed to be rebellious and ignore what was being preached, I failed miserably because of the music ministry. I love music. I always have. Music was the bait that made me consider the church, it made me pay attention. But my connection and relationship with this couple was what made me stay connected to the church.

I met her first. She was the praise and worship leader and I loved her voice and thought she was so beautiful. She could sing her butt off and I would mimic the way she held her microphone and led songs. I played that church cassette tape repeatedly memorizing all of her parts and ad-libs.

I met him as a result of her being his wife. They were the dynamic duo. He played the keys and bass and she sang. I thought, a match made in heaven. How awesome is that! They became my godparents. I wish I could say everything was easy like Sunday morning but it wasn't. From the age of 13 until now, we've had lots of great times and some not-so-good times.

Like the time when I was driving home from a gig in Baltimore and my car broke down. My godfather and I had made a pact that if I needed help I wouldn't call one of my male friends, but instead I would call him. So I took that opportunity to test it out. I called my godfather and he came and waited with me until the tow truck came and took me home.

Also, I remember the time when I decided to stay away from church because I was involved with my first romantic relationship

and thought I was in love. I couldn't knowingly sin and attend church too (I tried).
Though I took an absence from church and
stopped hanging around my godparents, my
godfather always called and maintained our
relationship. I remember times where my boyfriend was in the bed next to me, and I'd take
the call from my godfather. He would say, I
love you, I'm just calling to check on you and
let you know we are still here.

There are so many occasions that I can
recall my godparents rising to the occasion to
be the support system I needed. It's amazing
that my initial prayer was for a father, but I
got so much more in return. I got a father,
a bonus mom, siblings, and a newfound love
for families. Most importantly, it was clear
that God had heard and answered my prayers
beyond my imagination.

*****Beautiful Weirdo Nugget:** *Your idea of a prayer is cool. God's response to a prayer is GREAT. Remain open and expect to receive a response greater than your initial prayer. Prayers don't expire to those who believe.*

"Don't get me wrong
dinner and a movie
is fine
sometimes
And I dig
our conversations
they stimulate my mind
Not to mention
your sense of humor…
got me laughing uncontrollably
But there's one thing, that's missing
that's the most important to me
There's one thing, that's missing
that's the most important to me
I want a soul connection, connection
Not a soul disconnect…"

"Soul Connection"
Dosage I: Shades of Green

I HOPE THAT HE'S THE ONE

I've dreamed of being married since I was in the 10th grade. I wanted to be married so badly and felt that being married would give me the family unit I always wanted. At some point in time, every man I met was being considered as a candidate to be my knight in shining armor. Out of my potential candidates, there were two men who taught me lessons that impacted my perceptions on relationships.

Knight I

I was a sophomore in college, when I met him. We initially met because of a talent show. I sang a solo of a gospel song, and then we sang a duet of a popular R&B song. The crowd loved it! From that moment on we hung around each other and eventually became an item. Until then, I hadn't had a serious romantic relationship. It was the first time that I truly felt wanted by a guy and I wanted to keep him. I remember when I first met him; I laid out my dos and don'ts, to which he agreed. As the relationship moved forward, I became weak and my dos and don'ts were at war with my feelings of being wanted and not being lonely. He filled so many voids that I had as a result of being raised in a single parent family.

Over time, my emotions overwhelmed the need to maintain my morals. I started the relationship being sure of who I was and by the end of it I was a mess. He would mention things about me that he did not like, and I would try to change or stop doing those things for him. I remember him complaining about me singing all the time, so I stopped singing so much. There were a lot of things that I changed in hopes to keep things afloat with us. But after two years of a relationship, we had broken up, and I was devastated. This devastation lasted many years. Almost six years to be exact. I didn't know how to come to terms with being rejected and feeling unwanted.

I remember the last time I saw him (mistake #1). My visit with him was coming to a close and I was so proud of myself because I had abstained from having sex with him. For me, that meant I was finally over him. I shared this with him (mistake #2). So he turned up the heat and I faltered. The next morning he had gospel music playing because he knew how aggrieved I'd be because of my transgression. He had experienced it with me before. He knew me. I didn't cry in front of him. I gave him a letter and never saw him again.

I cried all the way home. I was sad because I had failed and because I heard the truthful words of my godfather echoing in my head, "Tekeah, why you keep messing with him, he don't love you." I learned the hard way that people who love you try, at all costs, to protect you. They don't intentionally mock you. Most of all, I cried to God and apologized for being such a flawed person. I remember asking Him how He could love someone like me... who continued to mess up. His response was simple, yet complex. He whispered, "I created you. You're beautiful. I love you. Flaws and all." Although it took me some time to heal from the damage I had inflicted upon myself, I gained a greater acceptance of my beauty. My beauty was, and is, solely based on the fact that God created me. He created me to be empowered.

***Beautiful Weirdo Nugget:** *Be who God created you to be. Don't dim your light to keep people around you. Love ignites, brightens, and expands your light. Love does not smother or extinguish your light.*

Knight II

The perfect type of man for me is tall, slender, black (so black that I could only see his pearly-white teeth). In my mind, I lived in the "perfect man" type of world, along with the fairytales of a damsel in distress being rescued by her knight in shining armor, and living happily ever after.

Then I met him. He was quick to burst my lollipop and bubble gum dreams. He was the most logical thinking man I had ever met. We discussed great topics and he challenged me to think differently about things. I remember I was talking to him about my weight. I was slowly gaining weight, yet I was in denial. So I complained about my weight and his response was, "Okay lose weight then. If you're not happy with your weight, do something about it." Was he serious? There I was talking about my weight problem and my dissatisfaction with my self-image, and he's telling me to lose weight. How crazy! At that time I was not appreciating his logic or his candor. I was fat but I didn't want to hear that I was fat. I wanted to be cajoled or pacified. But it didn't happen with him. That was one of many conversations where he met me with brutal honesty. Our relationship did not survive but wisdom from the conversations did.

A conversation that I will never forget was about romantic relationships. He told me, in a matter of fact tone, "People have fairytale realities when it comes to relationships and marriages and that's why they don't last. Instead of going into fairytale land, ask yourself, if this person never changed, could you deal with them for the rest of your life." When he presented this one question to me, it was eye opening and provided clarity for the gum and lollipops relationship land that I'd been living in. My view shifted and I was able to discriminate between the relationships that would be an investment and those that would be time robbers.

***Beautiful Weirdo Nugget:** *Relationships that are unsuccessful can still produce fruit if you are open to receive it. There are lessons in everything for those who are willing and open to learn.*

"Now this journey
it was hard
I had to look at my past
and look at some scars
that didn't heal
properly
as I was tryin
to move forward
I couldn't breathe…"

"I Believe"
Dosage 3: Choices

LOST ONE

It was April 2004 and I had just graduated from the University of Pittsburgh and was newly accepted into their Master's of Social Work program. Things were moving forward. I was semi-happy. Happy about completing my post-secondary education with an underlying quiet stream of depression, given my first significant relationship had just ended. So misery was the company to my recent achievement. I should have been high off life, celebrating a huge achievement, but I was not. Instead,

I moped around waiting for the fall session of graduate school to start.

During my break, I decided to travel to Philadelphia to see my ex-boyfriend. I was excited to see him, thinking that if we saw each other it would mend our relationship. I got on that Greyhound bus and made the trip. While on the way, I felt a nagging tingling in my breasts. I just thought it was a symptom that Mother Flo (menstrual cycle) would soon be here and I did not want her to ruin the occasion. So I took birth control pills in an attempt to stop Mother Flo from coming. It worked. That was about the only thing that worked during that trip.

My efforts to convince my ex-boyfriend to take me back as his girlfriend fell on deaf ears. But his ears weren't deaf enough for him to ignore the sound of our raging hormones. He heard that loud and clear. I was so naïve.

I thought that the sexual intimacy we shared meant that we were getting back together. Oh, foolish one. I returned home in an even deeper funk.

I made it home, yet the nagging tingling sensation in my breasts continued, but no menstrual. For some reason, I decided to get a pregnancy test. The positive sign on that test appeared at lightning speed. I took multiple double takes at the test, but that did not change the result. The utter shock and disbelief rested on my chest like a weight. I did not know what to do, but somehow I managed to gather the courage and accept that I was pregnant and move forward. I told those closest to me and some responses were dismal like "You have the rest of your life before you, don't mess it up – don't do this now" and others were like, "It's okay, you can do this."

And I did. I did it. I decided to move

forward and have the baby. I thought I had devised a master plan. I decided I was going to attend graduate school for the fall semester, have the baby during the spring semester, and then convince my grandmother to move with me to Pittsburgh for the start of my fall graduate semester. I had it all worked out. I accepted that I had made my bed and that I must take responsibility for my actions.

So I took the responsibility for the actions committed by my ex-boyfriend and I. After all, it was a couple of days before my undergraduate graduation; or was it after? I don't remember. What I do remember is telling my godfather what a great idea it was for my ex-boyfriend to support me and come up from Philadelphia to Pittsburgh to attend my graduation. Oh, foolish one. A simple invitation to my graduation, later led me to the campus medical center to get a morning after pill.

I went from disbelief, to acceptance, to preparation for having a child with my ex-boyfriend, to a doctor's appointment where they could not find my baby's heartbeat. I was devastated. I was eight weeks and one day pregnant, and that next week I had to have my baby removed. The pain and guilt I felt lingered past the removal of my baby. It resided deep within my core and was the silent conductor directing an orchestra of poor decisions that followed.

When I look back on some of the decisions I made following the loss of my child, it leaves me speechless. I had relationships with men so I would not be alone with myself. I revisited and revisited the relationship with my ex-boyfriend for six years following our initial break-up, trying to convince myself that I was over him or have him take me back. Six years. I had unprotected sex in some of my relationships because I was haunted by grief and loss. In some feeble attempt, my brain tried to fulfill that which was lost. I could go on and on about some of the poor decisions I made, because I was broken. It seemed as if I was on an endless merry go round playing a soundtrack of a looped lullaby of a baby's cry. It was torture.

Then one day after reading a book called "*The Shack*," that talked about children who had died, I decided to stop the torture. In that moment, I made a decision to let go instead of holding on and beating myself up in the process. I decided to stop self-sabotaging myself as payback for the loss of my child. It was only when I had decided that God was great enough to carry my burdens that I was able to live again without the agony of my baby's death being in the background of my mind. Instead of holding onto my baby,

I decided that it was okay to release him/her to be with God. Because carrying him/her around with me was slowly killing me.

***Beautiful Weirdo Nugget: *Mistakes are too heavy to carry around after they happen. Let them go. Repent, forgive yourself, and allow God to carry your mistakes and burdens so you can know peace and live again.*

"I spent time
on my hands and knees
praying to God
about the man of my dreams
I got an answer
and God said
seek me
And with that energy
he found me"

"Superman"
Beautiful Weirdo Mixtape

SUPERMAN

When I met my husband, I had no clue he would be in my future. As a matter of fact, I had just taken a whole year off from dating. Movies like *He's Just Not that into You*, diverse magazine articles about dating, and books like *Act Like a Lady, Think Like a Man* were all my new favorite forms of entertainment. With all of this newfound insight, I decided I was ready to date, but this time around I would only date to have fun. I didn't want to date with the goal of finding a husband, but

I wanted to enjoy my dating experiences and collect data on the things I liked and disliked. This was my own social experiment on dating, which yielded some pretty good ideals for my Pygmalion man.

I was having a blast dating when I received a Facebook message from a guy from my old elementary school. He had three kids in his profile picture and I couldn't help but wonder who this guy was, and especially with all these children. But like I said, I was dating for fun, however, I did make a mental note that he already had 3 children and he was only 28 years old. We started talking more and seeing each other every other weekend. I really enjoyed his company and felt that he enjoyed my company, too, since we had a lot in common.

So after three months of our dating, I did what seemed like the next step. I took a bold leap and told him that I wanted to date exclusively. That did not go over too well. He let me down softly by saying, "I'm flattered, but I'm enjoying being your friend." I will never forget that response. I felt embarrassed and I really didn't know how to regroup. My ego was bruised. I mean, I thought I was a good catch. I was single, a homeowner, I had a car, two degrees, and a good job. But he made it clear that he was only interested in friendship.

After consulting with my godfather about how to handle this situation, I was advised to continue being his friend. At that moment, I had a choice, rather to be his friend or to move on since my "biological clock" was ticking. I decided to accept the wisdom of my godfather and continued being his friend, which was one of the best decisions I have made in my life.

Although I didn't want to just be his friend, not rushing into a romantic relationship allowed us to really get to know each other. I was able to continue to observe and establish if I wanted something more than a friend in him. He was, and still is, a great friend. I believe our foundation of friendship enabled us to move on to an exclusive relationship, engagement, and then to marriage. That experience taught me not to throw away a friendship just because I didn't get what I wanted when I wanted it. I look back at the situation often and wonder how my life would've been had I chose not to involve myself with this friendship because of being rejected. I gained a true friend and I'm happy to say that I still have that true friendship in my marriage. He came at a time when I least expected it. I looked up in the sky, it's a bird, it's a plane! Oh, it's my Superman!

***Beautiful weirdo Nugget: *Don't throw away gems and treasures, because you aren't getting* *what you want when you want it. A treasure is a treasure; regardless if you are aware of it or not. It will gladly be someone else's delight.*

*"Wearin rose colored glasses
skewed your view
Got you thinkin
the world
revolves around you
Wearin rose colored glasses
you need to take them off
Take a good look at yourself
Pause"*

"Rose Colored Glasses"
Beautiful Weirdo Mixtape

THE OTHER WOMAN

My first vision of being married consisted of simple equations:

1) Single woman + single man + engagement = marriage,

2) Married couple + 2 year's time = children, and

3) Husband + wife+ children = happy family.

Simplicity at its best. If only my story was

that simple. Instead of having my simple equation, I had this:

Single woman + single man & three kids + ex-wife/other woman = complicated. I never once dreamed that my husband to be would have children, let alone an ex-wife. Never. But he did. And when we married, I gained his children and consequently interacting with his ex-wife, the other woman.

While I was dating my husband, I had some interaction with his ex-wife, which should have been a pre-cursor for what was to come once we were married. But for some reason, I thought this was just the treatment for being his "girlfriend." Surely things would change once we were married. How absolutely wrong was I? Completely.

I can recall when I first began dating my husband. Things were interesting between his ex-wife and I. She would deliberately ignore my greetings, a hostility I had to deal with head on. Not only would she ignore my salutations, but also if we were attending a basketball game with the children, she would purposely sit somewhere else. In addition to the previously mentioned behavior, there were instances where she would try to insert herself into our home and my marriage. I can remember countless occasions, where the kids would say to me, "Mom said," expecting her demand to be fulfilled in our home.

Adding fire to an already intense situation, she would send emails to address certain issues. If things did not go her way, she would get the kids to ask their dad, or she would personally ask him things when I was not around. It was horrible. This was not how I envisioned my relationship with her. I wanted her to like me. I wanted us to fulfill the vision I had in my head of being friends who enjoyed parenting together. In my mind, we were going to be like Jada Pinkett-Smith and Sheree Fletcher (Will Smith's ex-wife) who had a good relationship with each other. Nope. Instead I had "the other woman" trying to wreak havoc through our children and her past history with my husband.

After two years of putting my best foot forward to work together, I became angry and fed up. Instead of standing my ground and continuing to keep the right attitude toward the other woman, I just checked out. I stopped speaking to her and decided I had done enough.

Then my one of my sister-friends confronted me with a simple question, "Does God love her?" As I begrudgingly answered, "Yes," tears streamed down my cheeks as I was hit with the reality that we have all done things wrong, yet God still loves us. In that moment, a soft voice echoed inside of me asking, "What if I felt that I had done enough and checked out on you?" The tears that were initially a small spring had now graduated to a turbulent waterfall. I asked God for forgiveness right then and there. I am not better than the "other woman." I set up a meeting and apologized to her for my heart towards her. She in turn apologized to me. Our relationship is not a sunny walk in the park, nor have we gotten to the Jada and Sheree status, but one thing remains, I have not quit loving and I have not checked out.

***Beautiful Weirdo Nugget: *People will always be people. They will always have issues. Who they are and how they behave does not give you the right to stop loving them. Do not let people change your core of loving unconditionally.*

"It's a process
growin,
developin
It's a process
believin
and seein
It's a process
planting a seed
and reaping a harvest
It's a process
oh, yes it is"

"Process"
Greenteasoul

THE LADY WHO
LIVED IN A SHOE

When I was in the 10th grade in high school,
I had this dream that I would marry, have children, and live happily ever after. I would have
a nice house and maybe three kids. The vision
I had of my family would be just like what I
saw on The Cosby Show (minus two children).
My family would do activities together and
our disagreements would always be resolved
the same day ending with a smile and cuddle

time in the bed with my husband. Picture perfect. Yes that was my dream: husband, kids, house, a dog, and a cat for good measure.

If someone had told me that my future held a household size larger than that of the Cosbys, I would have laughed at them. I would not have believed it. In fact, even today, I am still in disbelief that I have superseded what I saw on The Cosby Show.

I am happily married with six children. SIX CHILDREN! So in total, we are, "the great family of eight." EIGHT! Eight is an assembly line of plates for our meals, a twelve-passenger van, budgets, juggling of everyone's needs, personal schedules, and family schedules. In addition, eight different egos, repeating the same instructions a million times a day, and lessons taught and unlearned. I could go on forever about our experiences and our adventures, but the list would be endless with never-ending roller coaster rides. With all of the highs and lows of family life, I have learned many beautiful weirdo nuggets from my children.

Episode 1: Communication

I have instructed my children on many things, all of which I think they understand the first time I have explained it. Well, if not the second time, I am sure that they understood by the fifth time. They did not. After a while of not getting the results I wanted and blowing up like a hot lava filled volcano, I tried something different. I posed some questions to myself: am I communicating clearly? Is something being lost in translation? Do my children understand what is being asked of them? I posed all of these questions to myself and realized that I was not communicating as clearly as I thought that I was. I would ask, "Why isn't your room clean?" I thought they would get the hint to clean their rooms. They did not. To them, that question is just a question and it does not contain any specific information. However, when I said, "I want you to stop what you're doing right now and go clean your room. And after you clean your room, you can watch television or go outside." It worked. Being time-specific got me the results I wanted.

***Beautiful Weirdo Nugget: *Weirdos have their own language and ways of communication. Sometimes your way of doing things needs to be tweaked for the population that you're communicating with. Keep tweaking until you get the results you want.*

Episode 2: Little Things

In the beginning of my marriage, I spent so much time correcting and laying down the law as it concerns our children. I was constantly telling them what not to do and what they had forgotten to do. I was stressed and frustrated and so were the children. I remember meeting with one of my mentors and she told me, "Relax girl, or they're going to hate you." The words, "hate me" wrung in my ear like a clanging cymbal. I did not want my children to hate me. I just wanted them to be great adults. I felt it was my job to train them to be great adults by correcting them consistently. I feared that they would not learn the lessons needed to become a productive member of society if I failed to correct them. I know, too deep right?

I was so stuck on making sure that I did not reinforce negative behavior that I forgot about the emotional component of the relationship. Then Holy Spirit compared the instruction tactics I was using with my children to those I've used with some of my best friends. Then Holy Spirit asked me, "Do you try to point out or correct every little thing in your friends' lives? What would happen if you did? You probably would not have them as friends." Point received. There should be a balance between the correction and the emotional development of a child. Not just with parent-child relationships, but also with any relationship. The children are not going to remember the sock that was found in the car that should have been in their hamper, but they will remember the good times – should you choose to create those times with them.

So, overtime I have improved as it concerns having a proper balance with my discipline. I do not have to nag and fuss over every little thing. I realize that my choice to sweat or not sweat the small stuff is not the deciding factor of whether their lives are going to head into a downward spiral. Furthermore, not nagging and fussing over every little thing leads to a more peaceful home and positively develops our relationship. This principle is one that has transcended every area of my life.

***Beautiful Weirdo Nugget:** *There will ALWAYS be something to gripe about, but at the end of the day…does it really matter? Is complaining about it contributing to your peace or to your frustration? Don't sweat the small stuff. Everything is not worth addressing.*

"You're beautiful
in every way imaginable
You're beautiful
from your head down to your toes
You're beautiful
in every way
I don't care
and
you don't care
what people say
cuz you're beautiful…"

"You're Beautiful"
Dosage 2: Choices

LOAF-A-BUTT

When I was in elementary school, my classmates taunted me with the words, "loaf-a-butt, loaf-a-butt!" If I focus enough, I can still see their facial expressions, hear their chuckles, and feel the sting from those words. Why did their taunt have such a sting? What's so harmful about repeating the words "loaf-a-butt" over and over to a classmate who was already uncomfortable with their self-image? So glad you asked. Let me paint this picture for you.

In elementary school, I was a short, pudgy girl. I wasn't allowed to show my fashion sense because we wore uniforms. Our school uniform was comprised of a gold peter-pan collar blouse with either a hunter green multi-colored striped romper or a solid hunter green skirt. I mainly wore the skirt that so eloquently highlighted my ample buttocks. The skirt made my butt look like it was its own personal shelf. Not to mention, upon seeing me, many adults made it a point to tell me that my butt sat on my back (thanks, community, for the support). Unlike adults, kids don't use neat little slogans like " your butt, is on your back." Instead, they are a tad bit more creative. Hence, the chants with the word "loaf-a-butt."

Loaf-a-butt is when your butt is described as being a loaf of bread on your back. So as I would walk over to greet my friends, I would hear some of the boys say, "Man her butt, looks like a loaf of bread." It was like my butt literally made an entrance before I had even spoke one word and I hated it.

But I managed and I survived elementary school. I silenced the hurt little girl inside and ignored what was being said because to cry about it would be an ultimate sign of weakness. I learned at an early age that people prey on the weak. I determined then, that I wouldn't be the prey and that I'd hold my head up high regardless of the whispers that made their grand entrance before me. I think that's where my issues with my weight began.

Over time, I began to take note that you were considered prettier if you were slender, and less attractive the more weight you gained. I remember conversations on the topic of weight and beauty and I recall comments such as, "Oh yeah, she's pretty for a big girl," as if being big discounted beauty. When my mother would talk to her friends about me, providing her friends with my latest developmental update, she would say, "Chile, Keah almost bigger than me." In the words of *In Living Color*, "Hated it!". Though I didn't comment on any of the messages that I was hearing, they soaked into my skin like ink on paper.

Instead of cowering or being shy about my weight, I did the opposite. I held my head high and boldly declared the love for my voluptuous parts. I loved my breasts which began as pebbles on the beach and at their biggest were 36FF, the blessed cup that runneth over. I took pride in my big butt and 42" hips as the women in my family are known for their big butts. I loved nakedness and I loved my body. I ignored any mention of needing a bigger size or any suggestions of needing different clothes from any of my close friends and family. I used a phrase, "This is me, this is who I am," to quiet their suggestions. I confidently sauntered in and out of the room with no evidence of a hurt little girl inside, though she was still there.

I didn't want to say that I secretly had issues with my weight gain. I didn't want to let on that sometimes I cried at night because I felt I wasn't pretty enough or because I wasted money on a gym membership that never saw my face. I didn't want to let on that I secretly admired skinny women and the fact that they seemingly could wear whatever they wanted and looked great in it. They didn't have to add the "loaf-a-butt" factor when considering skirts and jeans. I smiled and flaunted what I had because to give in and acknowledge that I was climbing the upward ladder of obesity meant that I was letting everyone who laughed at me in elementary school win. But then something changed.

A culmination of events led to an unforeseen path. The first thing was, I had quit my job as a program manager (assistant director) of a foster care agency. I decided that the job was contributing to my unhappiness. I was fat, not taking care of myself, and I wasn't singing as much as I wanted. Furthermore, I was unhappy because I wasn't making a change in the world like I wanted. After attending a music conference, where I was exploring rather to quit my job to pursue music full-time, I came to the conclusion that if you're unhappy about your life, do something about it. And so I did. I quit my job with the sole goal of exploring what made me happy.

Then, after I quit my job, I had the opportunity to take my Grahammy to some of her doctor's appointments. During one of her appointments, my Grahammy got on the scale, and at the age of 80, weighed 103 lbs. When I heard how much she weighed, I felt ambushed with an internal sucker punch. At that time, I was 29 years old, 5'3", and weighing 162 lbs. As the doctor was telling my Grahammy how he wanted her to gain more weight, I was stuck in a stupor. I thought to myself, "Your Grahammy weighs less than you. Are you going let your 80-year old Grahammy look better than you?"

As if that realization wasn't enough, the knockout blow came. In that same moment, I realized that I, at 29, was weighing 162 lbs., the same weight my Grahammy weighed when she was 62 years old and diagnosed with diabetes. Furthermore, much like having a big butt has a long-standing history in my family, diabetes does too. As I was processing all of this at my Grahammy's appointment, I decided that I had to get right, and tight, because I was not going to have my Grahammy looking better than me. Generations should get better with time not regress. I made the decision to change.

The change did not take place overnight. It started with a commitment to taking three group exercise classes at the gym. Later on, I incorporated the Weight Watchers regime, and I slowly began to see my body transform. More important than my body transforming was my mindset about exercising. The decision to commit to exercising yielded significant results. My energy level increased, a positive shift took place in my attitude about life, and most of all, I experienced dramatic improvements in my self-esteem.

When I initially attended fitness classes, I was unable to do push-ups or various other exercises, and within a short period I was doing push-ups at family gatherings as my talent in the family talent show. I found that exercise and movement contributed to my happiness. More than contributing to my happiness, it was a motivational stepping-stone of what could happen when I decided to make a change. That was the beginning of the journey to the road of doing what I love. Now, I am group exercise instructor with several certifications in different fitness areas. If someone would've told me that I would be a fitness enthusiast, I would have told them they had the wrong person. But it all started with a commitment to exercising three times a week.

The process of losing weight (I lost 48 lbs.), parallel with the issues of life. In life, I had ups and downs, times where I felt I was on top of things and other times when I didn't feel so hot. Just like my weight loss process, it was filled with peaks and valleys. Both situations led to the same crossroad; either you will keep going and striving for the best, or will you stop and allow yourself to go down the hill. During my journey, I decided that I would continue, regardless if I had gained or loss weight and I have applied that lesson to my life many times thereafter.

As for the little elementary school girl who overcompensated due to her insecurities, she has grown up. She no longer hears the laughter of her school classmates, but she hears her own laughter, and it's the sound of being genuinely happy.

***Beautiful Weirdo nugget: *When life seems like you're losing, don't stop. Continue. When life seems like you're winning, don't stop. Continue. Some movement is always better than none.*

"Look at me now
I'm mature and grown
I know
when to keep silent and when to say so
I know
when to hold on and when to let go
I know
when to take a stand and when to fold"

"After the Laughter"
Dosage 3: Time to B.E.

BEAUTIFUL WEIRDO

I have always wanted to be accepted, yet for most of my life I struggled with the idea of acceptance and rejection. In my heart of hearts, I wanted people to like me and enjoy my company even at the expense of cutting out the pieces that made me unique. I thought this feeling would subside as I got older, but I realize that the acceptance of self is a constant journey. I thought I reached a point where I had totally accepted my peculiarities and that this issue of being accepted would no longer rear it's ugly head and then came my experience as a member of a book club.

Book Club: Introduction

I had sought to become a member of this particular book club for a long time. Finally, after 12 years of waiting to get into this exclusive book club, there was an opening. I was so elated when I found this out. I'd just had my first biological child and thought this would be the perfect once a month outing. Not only was it an opportunity for me to get out of the house (breast feeding can hold you hostage), but it also combined two of my favorite things, reading and discussions. Things seemed to be going okay the first couple of meetings. Then I noticed undertones that were all too familiar. Undertones of "you're different...why are you here?" And their looks of disapproval were as if I was being scolded by my parents.

But I wanted to be in that book club so badly.

It was one of my dreams to be in a women's group discussing relevant life topics and gleaning from other women's strengths. I tried to make it work by ignoring what I was seeing, sensing, and feeling. A part of me was in denial, because I was in disbelief that I was experiencing this as an adult from other adult women.

After one meeting of being hyper-vigilant and analyzing every word that came out of my mouth so as to not offend others, I realized that being a member of the book club was no longer fun. Instead, this leisure activity had become a stressor. On the drive home from that meeting, I resolved that I would not continue to subject myself to stressful leisure activities or continue to be around people who did not honor the differences in others. Thus, I decided to terminate my stay as a book club member.

The decision to terminate my book club membership presented two options, to leave abruptly and without explanation ("drops mic" and exit) or leave and provide an explanation. I know some are from the school of thought that you don't owe anyone any explanation, but I felt that I did. And so I sent an e-mail sharing my feelings and what the book club experience was like for me. Why did I do it? I did it to bring awareness to how group dynamics can impact other's experiences in case they wanted to change the status quo when another person decided to join.

I think when we leave uncomfortable situations without giving the person feedback, we perpetuate a notion that its okay for them to continue doing what they have been doing. In essence, we reinforce their behavior. However, confronting the circumstance head on can lead to a crossroad where they can make a decision to continue on the same road or choose a different path. I don't know what road they decided to take, as I'm no longer in the book club. What I know is, that I did my best to positively end that chapter and to make it a better experience for the next person behind me.

Overall, I learned some important lessons: 1) who I am is a gift from God and I will not disgrace myself by being around people who don't honor or respect who God created me to be (awkwardness and all), and 2) my time is valuable and the time I allot for leisure activities should be fun and not stressful. When leisure activities become stressful, it's a sign that something needs to change.

***Beautiful Weirdo Nugget:** *Bullying exists in adulthood, be it physical or emotional bullying.*

Your acceptance of yourself is a journey and as long as you live, it will continue to be challenged. Continue to be a Beautiful Weirdo even when the masses are against you.

Book Club: Final Chapter

Following the termination of my book club membership, I had a vocal performance on the last Friday of the month, which would typically be a book club meeting night. In preparation for the show, I sent out Facebook blasts, e-mails, texts, and everything I could to let everyone know that I would be performing. I was excited and nervous at the same time, as the show was a marker of my return to the music scene (I had recently returned from hiatus.... remember I have six kids)! I had sent out so many promotions, alerting people to the performance that I really didn't know who was going to come.

I was sitting down, drinking hot tea, when the door opened and in came several ladies looking for seating together. To my surprise, it was the members of my former book club. They had come together to support me. I was so shocked, surprised, and happy that I greeted everyone with hugs. It was after hugging everyone that I realized that it was the last Friday of the month, the day of the monthly book club meeting. The fact that they decided to come together to see me perform spoke volumes. It was a gesture that said to me, I heard you and I support you.

As I sat there, preparing to sing my set, I was grateful that I didn't drop the mic and abruptly leave the group without explanation. Had I done so, I would have been robbed of seeing the beauty in the moment that I was now experiencing. The beauty of realizing that being true to oneself is always the way to go, no matter how uncomfortable it may be.

***Beautiful Weirdo Nugget:** *Always be true to yourself. Although, being true to oneself may not always FEEL good in the moment, don't let that feeling stop you from valuing yourself and reaping your reward. Being yorself has its own reward.*

ACKNOWLEDGEMENTS

God, I love you. You are my best friend and I'm so glad that I can be real with you (areas of improvement and all) and that you are soooo real with me. Thanks for being there with me through it all. My husband, Tron Mason, I am sure you are going to get a medal from God for marrying me. You have been with me through all of my ideas (there have been a million and I'm sure there are more to come), my tears, my joys, and my fears. You continue to hold me, esteem me, and challenge me to be the woman of God that I am and steadily becoming. I love you. My children: Tiarra, TJ, Jhiya, Ed, Trent, Royal, (Honour: he's not here yet, but this is for him too), I love you and want nothing but the best for you. You all challenge me to look at things differently and everything I do, I do, so that you know that anything is possible. To my parents: Mommy, Grahammy, Mom & Pop Brown, Mom & Pop Pop Montgomery, and Mom & Dad Plater, I love you to the moon and back and you will always get a return on the seeds that you have sown in my life. Thank you for your deposits in my life. To the best sisters in the world, Aiysha and Shelley, your love has transformed me to be a better person. I wish that everyone born would have friends like you in his or her corner. To my other sisters, you know who you are; you are always there and I am always gleaming from your light. I love you. To my pastors, Drs. Mike and Dee Dee Freeman and the entire Spirit of Faith Christian Center Family, thanks for always being in my corner and loving me through everything. To my editor, Iris, thank you for being there for me and providing your expertise (you rock)! To think we started this project over five years ago. To the photographer, Derrel Todd of Footprintstudios, you are magical. To Kia Darby of Yummy411 thank you for my flawless make-up. You are an artist and I've loved your work since the MaryKay bronzing beads. Tashawn Williams, thank you for being my hair doctor. To my Greenteasoul supporters who've been there for every performance and every CD made and purchased, thank you. To my fitness family and everyone who knows that I can make an exercise routine out of anything, "Some movement is better than none, wee hee!" To all of my clients who have allowed me to counsel you, "We are all teachers and we are all learners," thank you. To everyone who has ever supported me in any shape, form or fashion, be it a smile, a wave, words of encouragement, hugs, or if you just sent me positive energy, I appreciate you and thank you!

To all of the Beautiful Weirdos out there, enjoy who you are and who you are becoming. Continue to let your light shine and remember that you are not alone!

Beautiful Weirdos Unite

www.imabeautifulweirdo.com

Join our campaign **#iamabeautifulweirdo**

and e-mail your picture along with the

answer to these following questions to

tcmason@imabeautifulweirdo.com

Have you ever felt out of place, like you

didn't fit in?

How did you turn that awkwardness in to

beauty?

"Ain't no carbon copy here
I'm the only one
That God made just like me
Good looks and smarts
Don't fear
I've been designed so perfectly
And I love it
That I'm filled with faith
and that I'm filled with grace
Fearfully made
I love being me
Even with my flaws and all
I'm here to tell y'all
I'm a classic masterpiece
Even those who try
to spit on this design
end up losing their mind
cuz they see I'm still happy
You can't take my joy
You can't take my peace
What can I say
I love being me

"I Love Being Me"
Dosage 3: Choices

ABOUT THE AUTHOR

T.C Mason is a Washington, DC native who specializes in the total wellness of the individual. She utilizes clinical therapy, fitness (movement & exercise), crafts, and music (singer/songwriter) to assist and empower people to maximize their potential to be their best selves. She is a beautiful professional weirdo who believes in doing what she loves.

She received her master's degree in social work from the University of Pittsburgh and returned to DC and worked as a social worker for a number of years. T.C was promoted to program manager of a prestigious foster care agency, but resigned to pursue her happiness and music career. Since retiring from foster care, she continues to work as a clinical therapist, wellness and fitness consultant, and vocalist.

She has been in the mental health field for over 12 years and has a private practice where she counsels diverse populations: children, youth, individuals, couples, and families. She also teaches fitness classes and is a singer/songwriter who has recorded five albums and performs across the nation. She enjoys crafts and is a wife to a wonderful husband and mother of 6 children.

T.C utilizes her expertise in clinical counseling to facilitate different mediums to encourage people to accept and enjoy the beauty and uniqueness of their own peculiarities. T.C's passion is to help everyone to embrace their uniqueness. Afterall, we are all beautifully unique and so we are all beautiful weirdoes.

For more information about special discounts for bulk purchases, bringing the author to your live event/book club meetings, professional workshops, therapy, and speaking engagements, please e-mail tcmason@imabeautifulweirdo.com

Facebook: www.facebook.com/imabeautifulweirdo/

Instagram: imabeautifulweirdo

Twitter: @authortcmason

Website: www.imabeautifulweirdo.com

Lyrics in this book are excerpts from songs
featured on the following albums:

Dosage I: Shades of Green
Dosage II: Choices
Beautiful Weirdo Mixtape
Dosage III: The Time to B.E

These albums are available for purchase on
www.imabeautifulweirdo.com

www.ingramcontent.com/pod-product-compliance
Lightning Source LLC
Chambersburg PA
CBHW051728040426
42447CB00008B/1031